HOW TO BAKE

FOR BEGIN

ABSOLUTE GUIDE TO LEARN THE BASICS OF BAKING AND DECORATING CAKE FROM SCRATCH TO ADVANCE LEVEL

Copyright@2022

Jennifer Jackson

Table of content

CHAPTER ONE 3
   Step By Step Instruction To Bake A Cake 3
   Step 1- How To Make Vanilla Pound Cake 6
   Step 2 - Way To Build Chocolate Cake 11
   Step 3 - How To Make Apple Cake 20
   Step 4 - Subsequent Cake Recipes 28

CHAPTER TWO 40
   Instruction To Ice A Cake 40
   Step 1 – Fundamental Icing Method 40
   Step 2 - Layer Cake Icing Method 47

CHAPTER THREE 56
   Ways To Fondant A Cake 56
   Step 1 - How to Begin 57
   Step 2 – Roll And Use The Fondant 62

CHAPTER FOUR 70
   Instructions To Decorate A Cake 70
   Step 1 – Spreading Frosting Or Piping 71
   Step 2 - Work With Fondant 77
   Step 3 - Adding Fast Decorations 83

CHAPTER ONE

Step By Step Instruction To Bake A Cake

Nothing compares to the flavor of a cake baked in your own kitchen. Cake baking is as easy as measuring the ingredients, mixing them properly, and remembering to remove the cake from the oven before it burns. Continue reading to learn how to make three distinct cake flavors: vanilla pound cake, chocolate cake, and apple cake.

Materials Needed

- Measuring implements
- Hand or stand mixer
- Baking pans
- Toothpick (or wooden skewer)
- Spatula
- Oven
- Oven mitts or protective gloves
- Cooling rack

Ingredients

- ❖ The Vanilla Pound Cake
- One cup (225 g) of unsalted butter, softened (margarine).
- Use one cup (225 g) of granulated sugar.
- Use ½ teaspoon of salt.
- Use two teaspoons (9.9 mL) of vanilla extract.
- 5 eggs, room. Temperature
- Use two cups (240 g) of cake flour (or, you can use two cups minus two tbsp (234 g) of all-purpose flour plus 2 tbsp (16 g) of cornstarch)
- ❖ The Chocolate Cake
- Use 3/4 cup (170 g) of unsalted butter, softened
- Use 3/4 cup (64 g) of unsweetened cocoa powder
- Use 3/4 cup (90 g) of flour
- Use 1/4 teaspoon (1.4 g) of salt

- Use 1/2 teaspoon (1.2 g) of baking powder
- Use one cup (225 g) of granulated sugar
- 3 eggs, room temperature
- Use one teaspoon (4.9 mL) of vanilla extract
- Use 1/2 cup (120 mL) of buttermilk or sour cream

❖ The Apple Cake

- Use 3/4 cup (90 g) of flour
- Use 3/4 teaspoon (3.45 g) of baking powder
- Use 4 large apples, any variety
- two eggs, room temperature
- Use 3/4 cup (170 g) of granulated sugar
- The Pinch of salt
- Use 1/2 teaspoon (2.5 mL) of vanilla extract
- Use 1/2 cup (120 mL) of unsalted butter, melted

Step 1- How To Make Vanilla Pound Cake

1. Collect all of your ingredients.

Pound cake is one of the most straightforward cakes to make.

2. You should heat oven to 325 degrees Fahrenheit (163 degrees Celsius) and butter and flour a cake pan.

Pound cakes perform best when baked in deep pans such as loaf or bundt pans. Grease the pan with butter or shortening. After that, put a little layer of flour into the pan, flip it until evenly coated, and then tap out any excess flour.

3. In a mixing bowl, you should cream together the butter and sugar.

In a mixing bowl, combine the butter and sugar and beat until the mixture is light, fluffy, and creamy.

4. Add and stir in the eggs and vanilla.

To achieve the best results, add the eggs one at a time, beating the mixture between additions. Continue mixing the mixture until all of the eggs are included.

5. Add the cake flour and mix well.

Maintain a low speed on the electric mixer or use a wooden spoon to combine the flour a bit at a time until it is just incorporated. Take care not to over-mix.

6. You should pour the batter into the prepared pan.

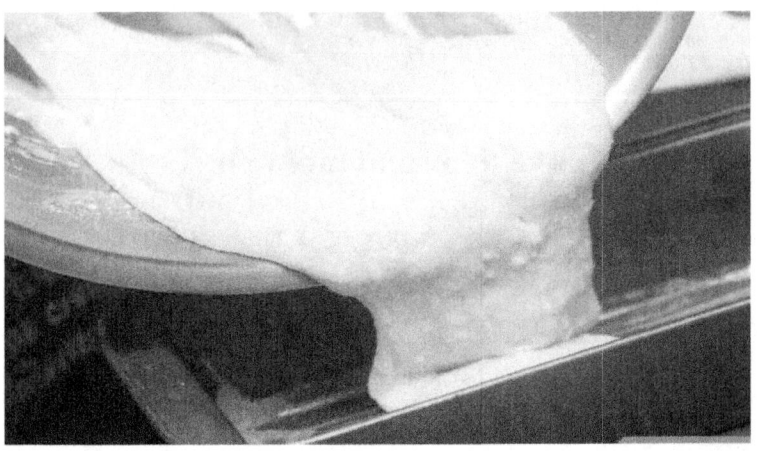

Scrape the bowl's sides with a spatula.

7. You should bake the cake for 1 hour and 15 minutes.

To achieve an equal bake, rotate the pan 180 degrees halfway through the cooking time. As soon as a toothpick put in the middle comes out clean, the cake is completed. Take pleasure in your delectable baked cake!

Step 2 - Way To Build Chocolate Cake

1. Collect all of your ingredients.

2. You should preheat oven to 340 degrees Fahrenheit (171 degrees Celsius) in addition to grease and flour a cake pan.

You can use a conventional round cake pan, a square baking dish, a loaf pan, or a bundt cake pan, or whatever you have on hand. Grease it well with butter or margarine to prevent the cake from sticking to the pan while baking. After greasing the pan, dust it with a light, equal layer of flour.

3. In a large mixing bowl, you should mix the wet ingredients.

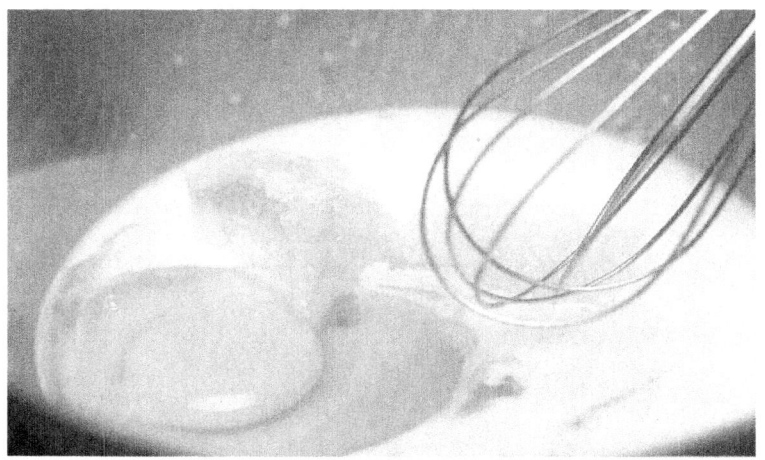

In a mixing bowl, You have to mix the butter, eggs, vanilla extract, sugar, and buttermilk. You should blend the ingredients thoroughly with a hand or stand mixer.

- In general, the "wet ingredients" in cake recipes are those that contain moisture. Sugar is frequently described as a wet component as well, despite the fact that it is not genuinely wet.

- Typically, the wet components are combined first in a large mixing bowl. The dry ingredients are combined separately and then combined with the wet ingredients.
- It is critical to follow the recommendations in cake recipes about the texture of the butter. If you use melted butter in place of softened butter, the cake may come out flat. The recipe calls for softened butter in this instance. You can plan ahead by setting out the butter while preparing the remaining ingredients, allowing it to come to room temperature.

4. In a separate bowl, you should mix the dry ingredients.

You should sift the flour, salt, cocoa powder, and baking powder into a small bowl. You should mix them thoroughly until properly mixed.

5. You should slowly add the dry mixture into the wet mixture.

On low speed, beat the mixture until the batter comes together and no white flour remains.

6. You should pour the batter into the prepared cake pan.

Scrape the sides of the basin with a spoon or spatula to ensure that all of the batter is transferred to the prepared pan.

7. You should put the pan into the oven and bake the cake for 30 minutes.

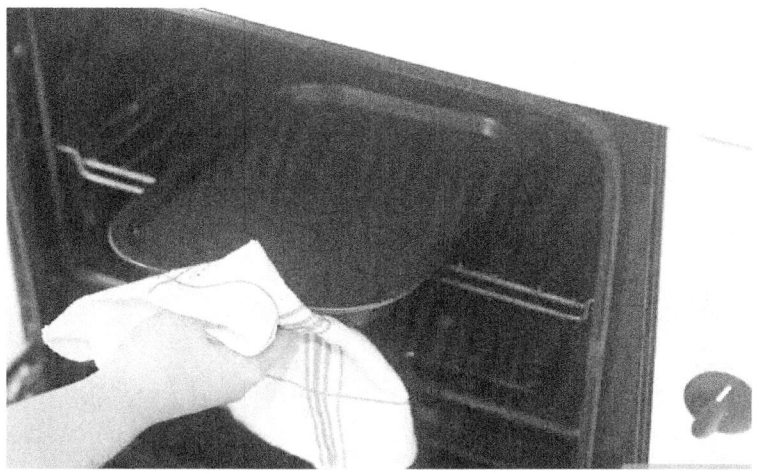

You may wish to place the cake pan on a baking sheet to catch any spilled batter. Halfway through the baking time, rotate the cake 180 degrees to achieve even cooking. When a toothpick put into the center comes out clean, rather than coated with batter, the cake is done.

- Monitor the progress of the cake on a regular basis to ensure it does not burn. However, you should do it through the oven window rather than opening the door, as this lowers the temperature inside the oven and may lengthen the baking time.

8. You should take out the cake from the oven and let it to cool totally.

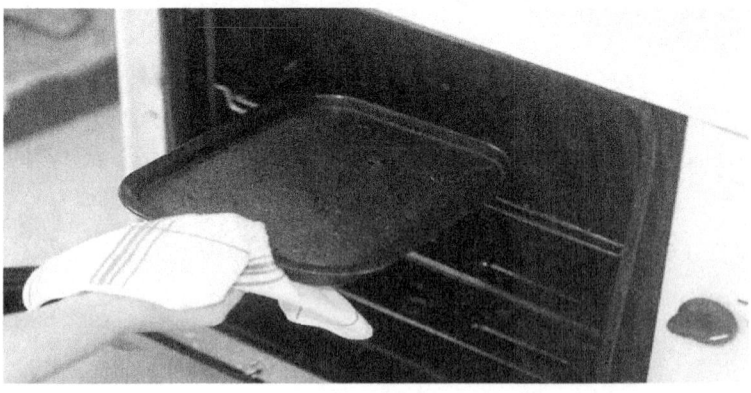

Place it on a cooling rack and cool for approximately 5 minutes before handling.

9. You should invert the cake onto a plate.

Utilize whatever dish you intend to serve the cake on.

10. Allow for thorough cooling before frosting the cake.

If you attempt to apply frosting to a heated cake, the frosting will melt and drip down the sides. Prepare a chocolate buttercream frosting, a simple buttercream frosting, or any other type of frosting. Enjoy!

Step 3 - How To Make Apple Cake

1. Collect all of your ingredients.

2. Grease and flour the cake pan and heat the oven to 350° Fahrenheit (177 degrees Celsius).

Use an 8-inch (20-cm) springform pan for this recipe; it has removable sides and is ideal for serving the cake during a party. Grease the pan with margarine or butter before flouring it to prevent the cake from sticking.

3. You should let the butter to cool after melting.

To melt the butter, you can either do so in the microwave or on the stovetop over a low heat. Allow it to come to room temperature before combining it with the remaining ingredients.

4. In a small bowl, you should stir the dry ingredients.

In a mixing basin, you should sift the flour, salt, and baking powder together.

5. Ready the apples.

Peel the apples with a knife or a vegetable peeler and then remove their cores. Apples should be cut into bite-size chunks (about 12 inch (1.3 centimeter) cubes).

6. You should blend the wet ingredients.

Cream the sugar and butter together using a hand or stand mixer. Then, add the eggs one at a time, mixing the batter between each addition. After that, incorporate the vanilla extract into the batter.

7. You should add the dry mixture to the wet mixtures.

You can choose to accomplish this by hand or use an electric mixer instead. You should stir the batter until it is smooth and creamy.

8. You should fold in the apples.

You should tenderly fold the apples into the mixture using a spatula. Avoid over-mixing the batter, which will result in a dense, stiff cake.

- Toss the apples in flour before adding them to the batter to prevent them from sinking to the bottom.

9. Cautiously pour the batter into the ready pan.

Smooth the top of the batter with the spatula to ensure it is equal.

10. You should bake the cake for just about 50 minutes.

Place the cake pan on a baking sheet to protect your oven from spills. After twenty-five minutes, you should rotate the pan 180 degrees. The cake is ready when the toothpick that is inserted into the middle comes out clean and the top of the cake has a golden brown color.

- Place whipped cream on top of the cake if that is what you would want.

Step 4 - Subsequent Cake Recipes

1. Before you start, make sure you have read through the list of ingredients and the directions.

It is essential to ensure that you have all of the necessary materials on hand. You don't want to be rushing to the store during the preparation process. If a necessary component is lacking, the finished result could not turn out as expected.

2. The cake pans should be prepared.

Ascertain that the pan is the correct size or shape. While bundt cakes must be prepared in bundt pans, other cakes can be baked in a range of sizes. Grease the cake pans to prevent the cake from sticking. On a piece of paper towel, apply half a tablespoon and seven grams of butter, margarine, or vegetable shortening and rub it all over the inside of the pan. On top, sift approximately 1 to 2 tablespoons (8 to 16 grams) of flour.

- Add a little amount of flour to the pan, rotate it to ensure even coverage, then shake and dump off any excess flour before setting the pans aside.

3. You should preheat the oven to the temperature specified in the recipe.

Ensure that you follow the instructions exactly, as adjusting the temperature higher or lower may cause problems.

4. Use the most precise measurements of ingredients and add the components in the order specified.

The majority of cake recipes begin by combining wet components (such as eggs, oil, and milk), followed by dry ingredients (such as flour, baking powder, cocoa). Prior to adding the components to the main bowl, perform any necessary preparations such as sifting, whisking or beating, and packaging.

5. Mix the cake batter according to the directions on the recipe.

Certain recipes can be mixed using either a stand mixer or a hand mixer. Be cautious, as instructions may urge you to use a rubber spatula to fold in flour or other ingredients. While mixing, scrape down the sides of the basin occasionally with a spatula or spoon to ensure that everything is fully mixed.

6. You should evenly pour the batter in the prepared pans.

Fill the prepared pans two-thirds full, as the cake will expand during baking. Tap the cake pan gently on the counter to dislodge any large air bubbles in the batter.

7. Arrange the pans on the preheated oven's center rack.

In case any of the batter bubbles over, you can place the cake pan on top of a baking sheet ensure that the pans do not touch the wall of the oven at any point.

8. Shut the oven door and immediately set a timer for the baking time given.

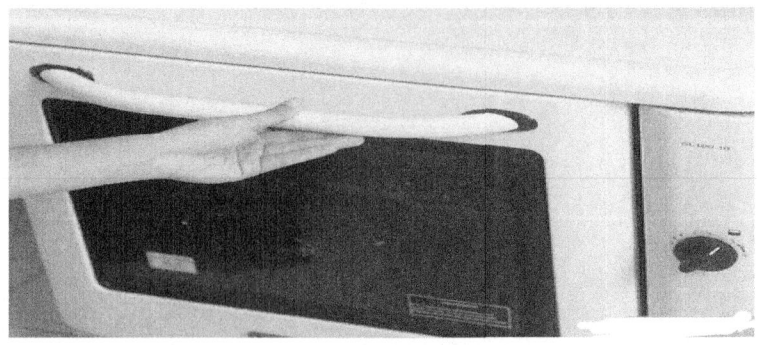

If a time range exists, use the median or middle value (bake it for 35 minutes for a range of 34 to 36 minutes or 53 minutes for a range of 50 to 55 minutes). By using the median, you can ensure that the cake does not over- or under-cook.

- Resist the impulse to open the oven door during baking, as this allows heat to escape and may result in an unevenly cooked cake. Turn on the oven light and inspect via the oven glass, if applicable.

9. Inspect the cake and check for doneness.

Insert a toothpick or wooden skewer gently into the cake's center. The cake is ready when a toothpick inserted into the center comes out clean or with only a few crumbs stuck to it. If not, return it to the oven for an additional 3–4 minutes. Continue testing for the same period of time until the correct result is obtained.

10. Remove the pan from the oven and cool for 15 to 30 minutes on a wire rack.

To loosen the sides of the pan, run a thin spatula around the perimeter. Arrange the wire rack on top of the pan, flip it, and lightly tap it to release the cake.

- Allow it to cool completely before decorating, since heat will cause frosting and icing to dissolve.

Tips

- When a hot cake is attempted to be removed from the pan, it may crack and fall apart.
- Check with a toothpick to verify if it is completely done.
- Verify your measurements twice before transferring them to mixing bowls. A few teaspoons of additional or missing flour might have dramatic and unintended consequences on the completed cake.
- You should prevent over-mixing the batter.
- If you're using another recipe, follow the guidelines specified in that recipe.
- Always butter the cake pan generously.

- When a recipe calls for room temperature ingredients such as butter or cream cheese, unwrap the item and set it in a bowl on the counter for 30–60 minutes to soften. You can determine its softness by probing it with a fork or your finger.
- To make it vegan, replace the butter with vegetable oil or melted coconut oil. Substitute applesauce for eggs; for example, replace 1 egg with 14 cup (59 mL) applesauce.
- Ice the cake after it has cooled completely. This can result in the crumbling of the cake and the icing running to the sides or sliding off the cake.
- To ensure equal heating and the best results, use high-quality, heavy-duty aluminum baking pans.

Warnings

- Because oven temperatures vary, keep a close eye on your cake to prevent it from over baking.
- When opening a hot oven, take care to keep small children and pets out of the way.
- To avoid burns, always use oven mitts or protective gloves when removing the cake from the oven.

CHAPTER TWO

Instruction To Ice A Cake

If it's a chocolate, lemon, or carrot cake, this delicious confection must be iced. While a finished cake will taste fine regardless of how it is iced, there are a few tips to follow if you want it to look attractive. Continue reading to learn how to frost a basic or layer cake.

Step 1 – Fundamental Icing Method

1. Place the cake on a platter.

It is recommended to ice the cake on the same dish that will be used to serve it, as it will be difficult to shift the cake to a separate plate once it has been frosted.

2. Let the cake to cool totally.

If you attempt to ice the cake before it has cooled completely, the icing will melt, destroying the texture. Allow it to reach room temperature before touching it with your finger.

3. In a bowl, place some confectioner's sugar.

A cup or so of confectioner's sugar is required for a 9-inch (22.9-cm)-diameter cake. You can always make more if necessary.

- Use confectioners' sugar instead of granulated sugar, as it is too coarse and will result in a grainy-textured frosting.
- Additionally, other sugars, such as brown sugar, are not allowed for icing.

4. You should boil a cup of water.

You should stir a teaspoon of hot water into the sugar until it reaches a smooth, spreadable consistency.

- If the icing becomes too thick or lumpy after adding the first teaspoon of water, add another teaspoon of water. Continue churning and adding small amounts of water until the mixture reaches the desired consistency.
- Add extra confectioner's sugar if the frosting gets too runny after adding too much water.

If the mixture seems to be excessively thick, you can add little water it.

5. Add in color and flavor.

If you want to personalize the color or flavor of your frosting, simply add a few drops of food coloring and flavoring. After methodically mixing them into the frosting, you should keep putting color plus flavoring to the icing until it obtains the color and flavor that you want.

- Popular flavors include vanilla, almond, hazelnut, peppermint, and others. These are

available at a variety of grocery stores, and even large options are available at bakeries.
- Be cautious not to put in a put in more quantity of color or flavor, as just a small bit can go a very long place. You should place in 2 or 3 drops, give it a mix, then taste it as well as look it over before putting in any other.

6. Ice the cake.

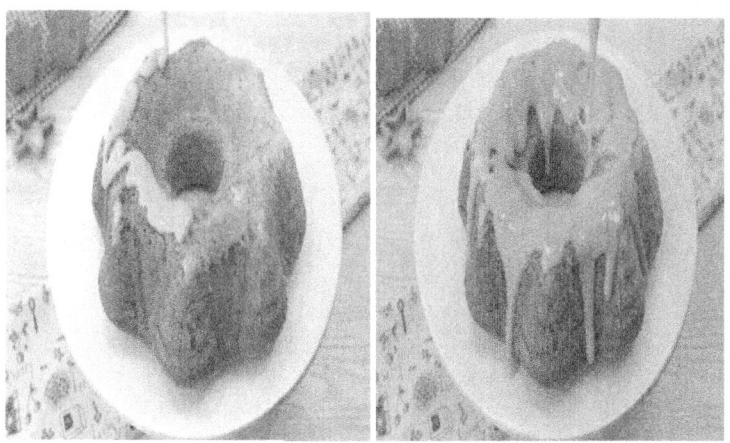

To decorate the top of the cake, use a spoon to spread some icing over it. In the same way that you would butter a piece of bread, spread it out evenly with a butter knife. You should put it in mind to spread frosting on both of the edges along with top of the cake.

- To even out the texture of the icing, first submerge the knife in warm water, then shake off any excess water, and use the knife.

7. You should arrange the decorations on the cake.

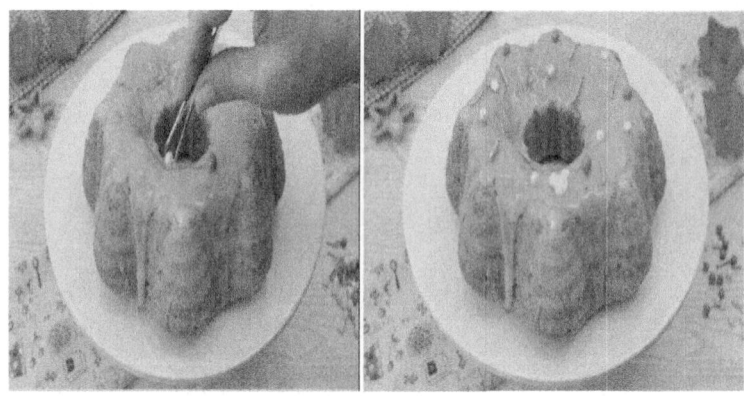

Sprinkles, marzipan models, plastic characters, and birthday candles, for example, can be added. Baking supply stores provide a plethora of options.

8. Allow it to set.

Refrigerate the cake to allow the icing to completely set. It will be ready to eat in about a half hour.

Step 2 - Layer Cake Icing Method

1. Bake two equal size cake layers.

You may decide round or square cakes, but the proportions must be identical. You should let it the cakes to cool thoroughly.

2. You should turn one cake onto a platter.

Due to the cake's ungainly nature once layered and iced, it's preferable to use the same plate that you intend to serve it on.

3. Trim the cake's circular top with a long serrated knife.

Slice approximately 14 inch (0.6 cm) from the top of the cake with the knife parallel to the brim.

- Slice straight across, maintaining a flat knife throughout.
- Make an attempt to produce a flat, level surface. This will act as the foundation for the second layer.
- Remove the cake's rounded top and discard it, or keep it to consume.

- Avoid cutting the cake's top with a little knife, as this will result in an uneven surface.

4. You should spread the filling over the cake layer.

Fill the bottom layer of the cake with the filling of your choice. Spread it evenly with a spoon or a knife until it covers the entire layer.

- Popular cake fillings include raspberry, lemon curd, cream, and chocolate.

- Avoid allowing the filling to leak over the borders, since this will cause it to combine with the icing.

5. You have to put the second cake layer on top of the first.

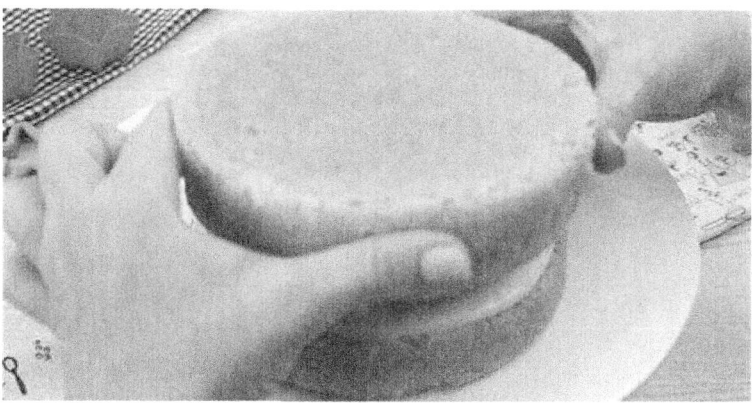

In the second layer, the side that is flat should be facing down, and the side that is rounded should be facing up.

- If you prefer a flat surface for the finished cake rather than a domed one, repeat the process of slicing the rounded top of the second layer with a serrated knife. Place the cut side down so that the cake's top is formed by the smooth, flat bottom of the second layer.

- Wipe away excess filling with a paper towel as you add the second layer.

6. The cake should be ice with a crumb cake.

In order to achieve the polished appearance of a professionally made cake, you will need to apply two layers of icing. First, you will apply a "crumb coat" that will serve as a foundation for the second layer, collecting any crumbs that may have fallen through the first layer and ensuring that the second layer will appear smooth and free of crumbs.Ice the cake with a butter knife using the instructions above or your own frosting recipe.

- The crumb coat does not have to be flavorful or colorful, unless you choose it to be. Alternatively, you can use simple white icing.
- Make certain you cover the whole cake with icing, including the sides. Take care not to overfill the icing with filling.
- It is acceptable if the crumb coat does not appear ideal; the goal is to completely cover the cake and capture the crumbs.
- You should allow half an hour for the crumb coat to set before continuing.

7. You should ice the cake with a last layer of icing.

Ice the cake once again with the instructions above or your own icing recipe.

- You should add flavor and color to the batch of icing used for the final layer if desired.
- Decorate the cake with fresh fruit, flowers, or other toppers and leave aside until set before serving.

8. Completed.

CHAPTER THREE

Ways To Fondant A Cake

So you're interested in fondanting a cake but have been told it's too difficult? With practice and knowledge, you'll be able to fondant a cake easily and produce a stunning display.

Things You'll Need

- String
- Rolling pin
- Smooth, clean surface to work on
- Knife or pizza cutter
- Fondant smoothing tool (optional)

Ingredients

- Buttercream
- Fondant
- Cake
- Powdered sugar (or cornstarch)

Step 1 - How to Begin

1. Prepare and set aside your buttercream.

Then, use a piece of twine, measure the top and sides of the cake. Wrap a long piece of string around the cake's top and fold the ends against the cake's sides. Remove any excess string that comes into contact with the plate. Remove and set away the string. You're going to use it to determine the size of your fondant.

- If you're making a multi-tiered cake, take measurements for each tier separately.

- For any other cake, measure the maximum width across the top (diagonally from corner to corner for a square or rectangle cake) and multiply by two.

2. Using a palette knife to cover the cake with a thin layer of buttercream.

The buttercream will aid in the adhesion of the fondant to the cake, so be sure to cover the top and sides of the cake with it. Make the surface as smooth as possible; any irregularities will be visible. If the cake has any cracks or holes, fill them in with buttercream and smooth it down.

- Consider using a cake decorating turntable to simplify and expedite this procedure.
- Additionally, you can substitute light or dark ganache or apricot jam for the buttercream.

3. You are going to want to chill the cake in the refrigerator for half an hour.

This will allow the buttercream to firm sufficiently. The fondant will slide right off if the buttercream is too soft.

4. Clear the area with a broom and then dust it with powdered sugar to create a large, smooth working surface.

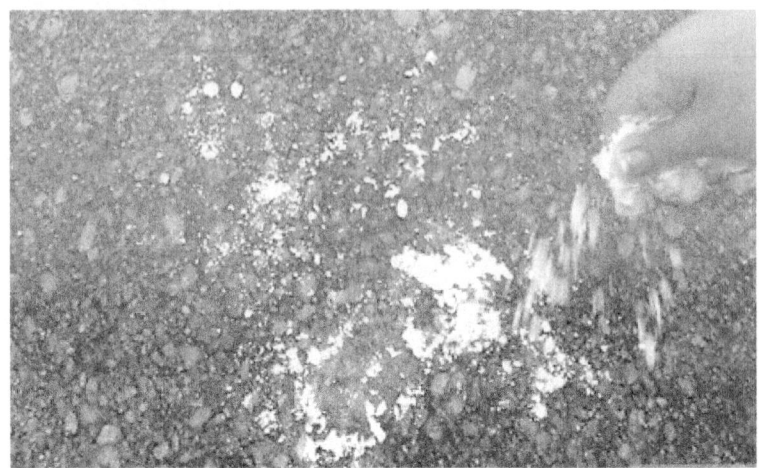

The surface must be smooth, as any irregularities will show through the fondant. Dusting the work surface lightly with powdered sugar can help keep the fondant from sticking.

- Make a paste consisting of one part cornstarch and one part powdered sugar if the air in your location has a high humidity level. It might be a good idea to add a very thin layer of vegetable shortening to the surface if it is extremely dry.

5. Before you use your fondant, let it get to room temperature first.

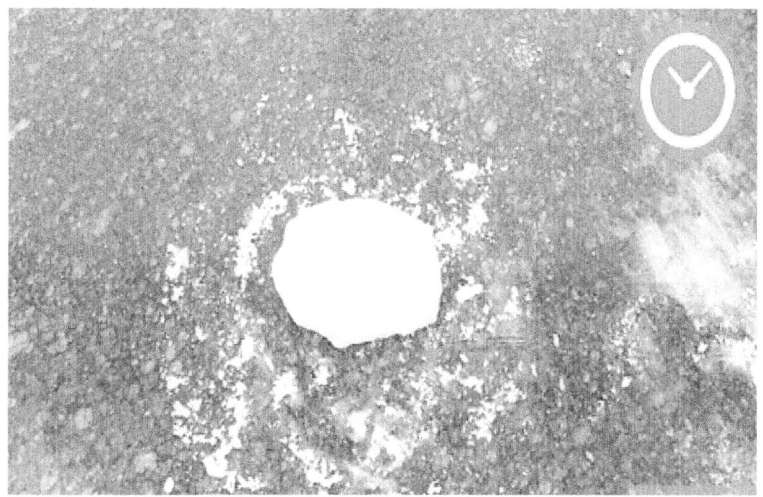

This makes it more manageable. You can knead it for about five minutes to soften it and make it easier to deal with; however, do not allow it to get too soft and sticky.

- During the process of kneading, you could like to experiment with adding some colored icing gel or paste. Instead of a liquid food coloring, use a food coloring that comes in powder form.

Step 2 – Roll And Use The Fondant

1. Using your hands, press the fondant into a shape that resembles a rough pancake.

Make it not too thin yet. Flatten the fondant into a square or rectangular shape if you are covering a square or rectangular cake.

2. Roll out the fondant to a thickness of approximately 1/4 to 3/8 inch (0.64 to 0.95 cm).

Turn the fondant 180° every several minutes while rolling it out. This will assist in maintaining a circular and equal shape. Avoid lifting and flipping the fondant, since this will cause it to rip.

3. Using the piece of string to measure the fondant.

Lay the rope you previously cut across the fondant. The fondant should be the same size as the string or slightly larger; any excess fondant can readily be trimmed off afterwards.

4. Roll the fondant loosely onto the rolling pin.

Roll the rolling pin from one end of the fondant to the other, gathering up the fondant as you go. This will aid in the transfer of the fondant to the cake and minimize the likelihood of it ripping.

- Before attempting this, lightly dust the rolling pin with powdered sugar.

5. Unroll the fondant gently over the cake.

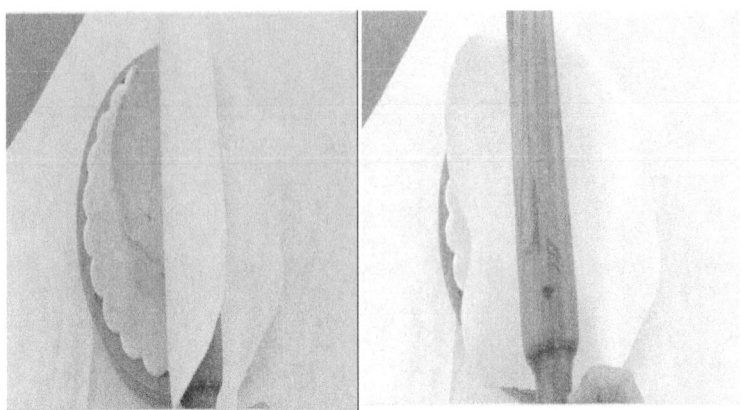

Roll the rolling pin around the top of the cake, close to one of the edges, unwinding the fondant as you go.

6. You should smooth the fondant on top of the cake.

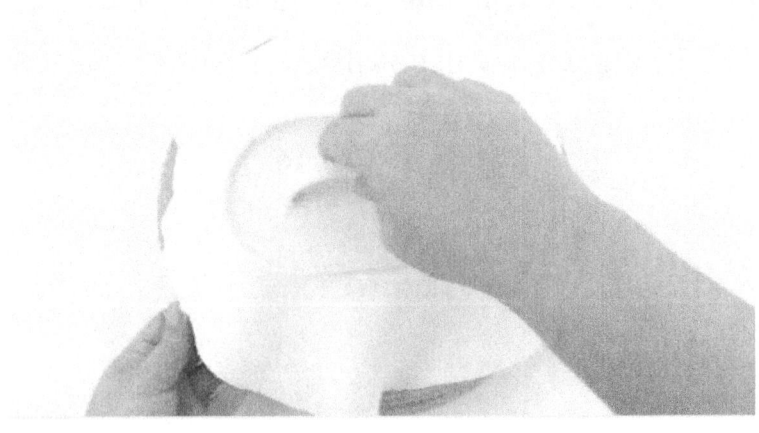

Utilize your fingertips to start at the top then work down the sides of the object. Check for creases, wrinkles, and air bubbles. Any surplus fondant should be trimmed away. Use a knife or even a pizza cutter to cut the dough. Cut as near to the cake's bottom as possible.

7. Complete the smoothing of the fondant.

You may give your cake a polished appearance by "ironing" the surface of the fondant using a glass with a flat side or a fondant smoothing tool. This will help you obtain a smooth finish.

- Bring out its luster by giving it another brushing after giving it a mist of cooking oil and lightly sprinkling it.

8. You have to complete the cake's decoration.

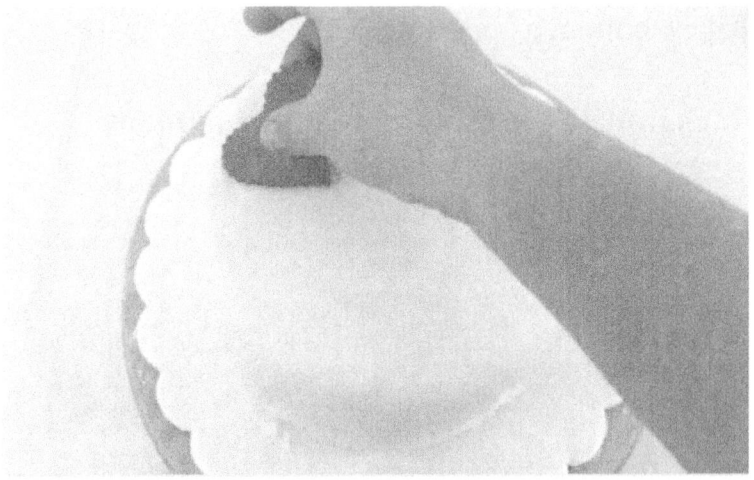

You have the option of leaving the cake unadorned, or you can adorn it with embellishments made of buttercream frosting, such as flowers, swirls, or calligraphy. In addition, you can add design to your fondant by working with embossed silicone gel mats.

9. Completed.

Tips

- Cover the fondant when not in use to prevent it from drying out.
- To prevent drying, store the fondant curled into a ball and sealed with oil and plastic wrap.
- Use one batch of Marshmallow Fondant to make a smaller cake. To make a larger or multi-tiered cake, divide the batter into two or more batches. Always overestimate.

CHAPTER FOUR

Instructions To Decorate A Cake

Decorating a cake is one of the most enjoyable and distinctive aspects of the cake-making process. If you are a novice decorator, begin with easy techniques such as creating simple designs on frosted cakes or topping them with embellishments. Cover the cake with fondant and mould the material into intriguing textures for more experienced decorators. Experiment with cake decorating until you uncover your preferred abilities!

Step 1 – Spreading Frosting Or Piping

1. Decide on a cake frosting.

Use any frosting that is thick enough to adhere to the cake's top and sides. If your frosting is too runny to pipe or spread with an offset spatula, gradually add powdered sugar until it becomes thick enough to pipe or spread. Consider the following:

- Buttercream, often known as Vienna cream
- Cream cheese frosting
- Frosting with marshmallows
- Royal Icing

- Swiss meringue buttercream or Italian meringue buttercream
- Ganache

2. Use an icing smoother to make evenly frosted side.

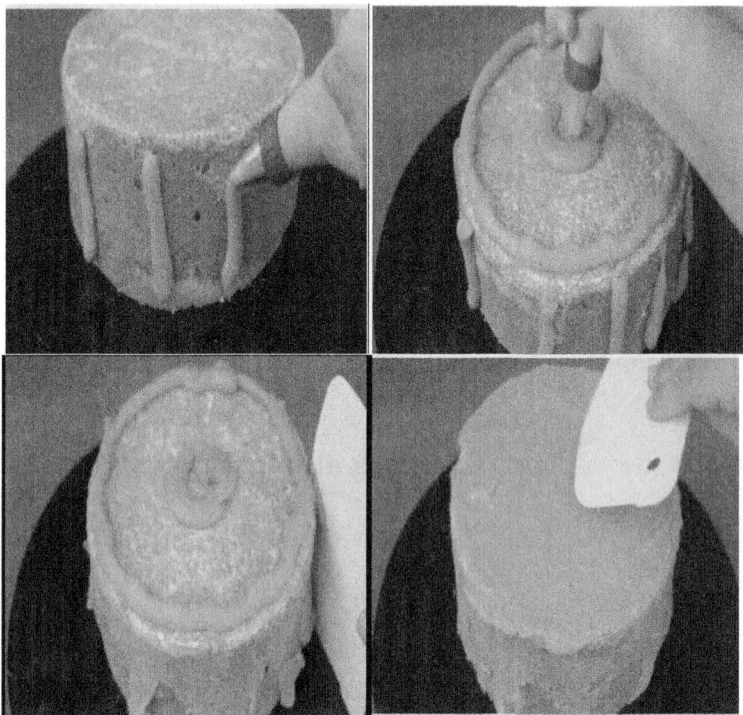

Pipe thick bands of frosting around the sides of the cake using an icing tip and a pastry bag. Continue up the sides until they are completely covered with icing. Then, vertically press an icing smoother or bench scraper against the cake's side. Smooth the smoother all the way around the cake to get a uniform surface.

- If the cake is on a turntable, it is easier to use the icing smoother. Then, while holding the icing smoother against the side, slowly rotate the cake.
- If you prefer to leave the sides of the cake "bare," put a few tiny areas of frosting along the sides to reveal the cake layers.

3. Fill a piping bag with royal icing and pipe a pattern onto the cake.

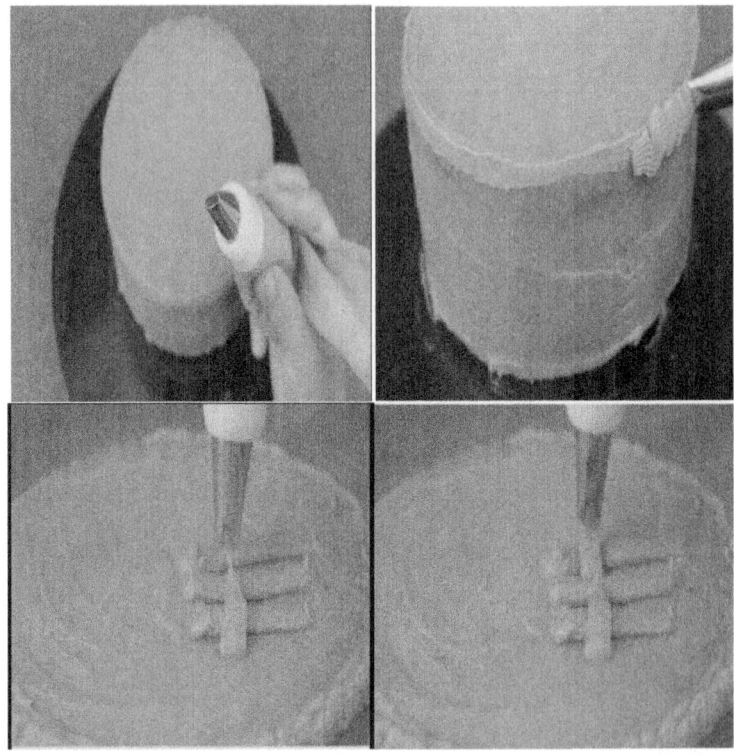

Choose a piping tip that will assist you in creating the desired design. For instance, use a petal tip to pipe a ruffled edge along the cake's perimeter, or a plain round tip to pipe dots on the cake's top.

- If you do not have a piping bag, transfer the frosting to a food-safe plastic bag and snip off the bottom tip. While you will lose control over the level of piping detail, you will receive a simple piping bag.

4. Create decorative shapes, flowers, or words with piping tips.

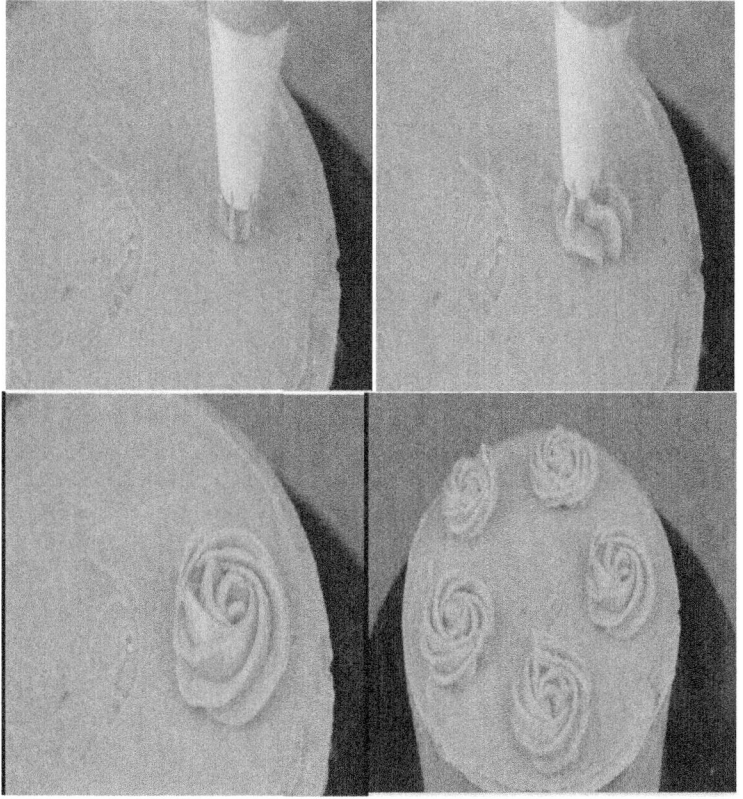

Once the cake is completely covered in the icing of your choosing, decide whether or not to add a few embellishments. Alternate the tip on the piping bag to create words or flowers. Certain points are shaped specifically for certain objects, such as leaves.

- For instance, to create beautiful fleurs-de-lis, pipe three reverse shells using a star tip. Additionally, you can pipe the frosting into a simple rosette using the star tip.

5. You should swirl the frosting with the back of a spoon.

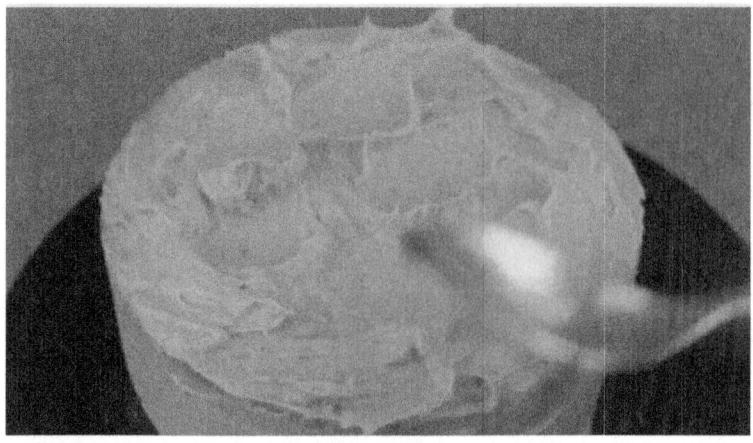

Assure that the top and sides of the cake have a minimum of 1 to 2 inches (2.5 to 5.1 cm) of frosting. Take a spoon and hold the back in such a way that the tip is softly pressing into the frosting. To make a wave, twist the spoon in a half-circle motion. Carry on in this manner around the sides and top of the cake.

- To create an easy zigzag design, pull the tines of a fork back and forth through the frosting.

Step 2 - Work With Fondant

1. You should cover the whole cake completely to make sure a even surface.

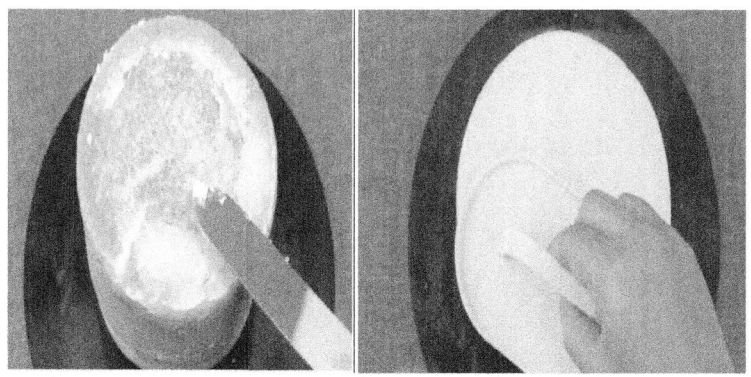

You can produce the smoothest possible surface for your cake by purchasing or preparing fondant.

The fondant should have a thickness of approximately 14 inches when rolled out on a work surface dusted with powdered sugar (0.64 cm). Position the circle of rolled fondant on top of a cake that has only a light coating of frosting. Then, use a motion similar to that of smoothing spread the fondant over the top and sides of the cake to ensure that it adheres.

- The crumb coat of frosting will help the fondant adhere to the cake, which is an important step in the process.
- You should always trim the excess fondant away from the bottom edge of the cake. Conserve the remnants and use them to create more decorations.

2. You should apply fondant fringe, ribbons, or swag.

Cut pieces of fondant and trim them into fringe to add texture to the cake. Then, down the sides of the cake, drape the fringe or roll and drape the fondant. Additionally, you can fold fondant strips to form ribbons or bows. Attach them to the cake's top or sides.

- Make a single, huge bow and set it on top of the cake for a striking look. Make multiple rows of vividly colored fondant fringe if you want a colorful cake. Wrap these around the cake's sides.

Tip From Expert

I've always believed that fondant is excellent for creating accent decor, whether it's flowers, borders, or something else. In terms of eating a cake, I believe that people prefer various types of icing. If you wish to cover the entire cake, frost it first to ensure the fondant is adhered to something. That way, people may eat the icing they want underneath!"

3. You should shape fondant into flowers or figures.

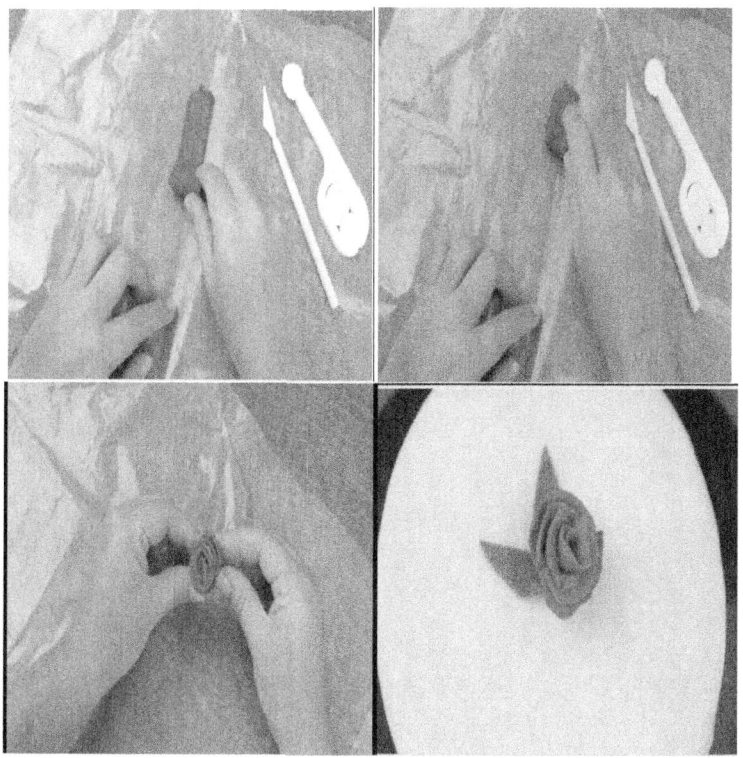

Roll a piece of fondant and cut it into long strips to create a flower. Wrap the strip tightly around itself after folding it in half. Then squeeze the flower's base and adhere it on the cake. Additionally, you can use fondant to construct any shape you like, including a person, animal, or plant.

Tip: Roll a piece of fondant and press impression molds, lace, or leaves onto it to create fondant impressions. Remove the item to reveal a decorative fondant piece that can be affixed to the cake.

4. Paint the fondant with an image or design.

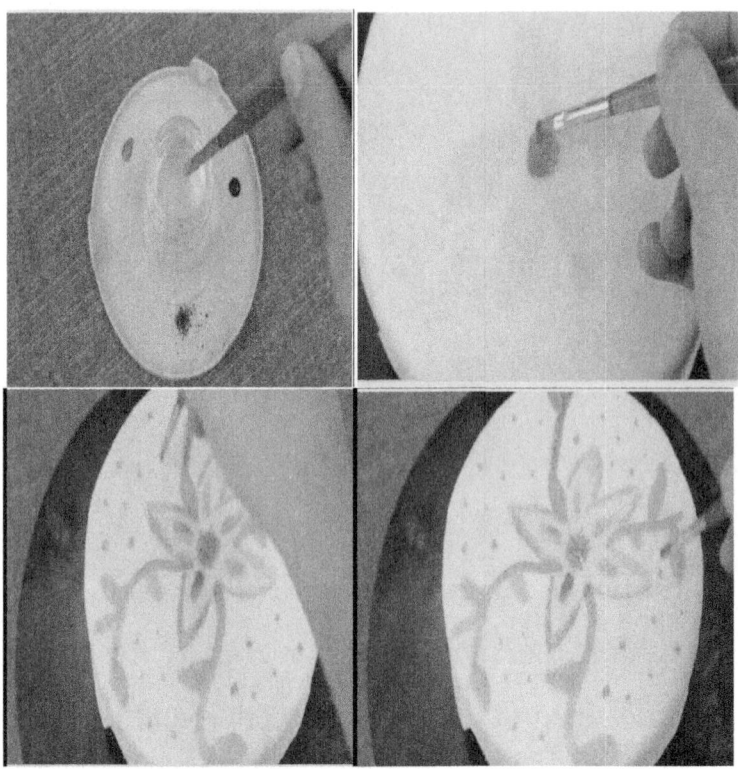

In a small dish, combine a few squirts of vodka and a few squirts of gel-paste food coloring to create a simple food-safe paint. Then, using a fine paint brush, paint the fondant's surface. It's simple to make abstract designs or to devote considerable time to painting a particular motif.

- Stippling is a simple way to produce an effect. In the paint, dip a medium-sized brush with stiff bristles. Then, using your finger, press it into the fondant to create a dot. Continue creating dots around the cake's sides or top.

Step 3 - Adding Fast Decorations

1. Place fresh flowers on the cake's top or sides.

Purchase pesticide-free flowers and gently place the stems into the cake to provide an elegant or rustic touch. To prolong the life of the cake, wrap the stems in an edible sealer before inserting them. Among the edible flower varieties are the following:

- Chamomile
- Marigolds
- Carnations
- Cornflowers
- Daisies
- Fuchsia
- Hibiscus
- Pansies
- Roses
- Lavender

2. You have to add crunchy or chewy textures to the top of the cake.

You should sprinkle sprinkles, chopped nuts, caramels, meringues, or candy over the top or sides of the cake to cover the icing or to create a burst of color and texture. To adhere them to the cake's sides, gently press them into the frosting with your palms.

- Toffee or spun sugar creates a visually stunning adornment with a subtle crunch.

Tips:

- For a tropical-themed cake, use shredded or colored coconut flakes.
- Sort candies according to their hue and arrange in a rainbow arrangement.
- Combine two mini-candy canes to form a heart.

3. Learn to decorate the cake with a topper or figures.

When decorating a wedding cake, the bride and groom may request brides, grooms, bells, or hearts on top. Choose robust toppers or figurines that will not sink too deeply into the cake. Bear in mind that wedding toppers and sculptures are not exclusive to weddings. For instance, you can adorn birthday cakes with clean:

- The Toy Animals
- Action figures
- Little plastic dolls
- The Toy cars

4 Arrange the fruit on top of the cake.

Utilize whichever fruit is in season and complements the cake's flavor. For instance, if you're making a summertime lemon cake, garnish it with fresh blueberries, blackberries, or strawberries. If you're making an autumn gingerbread cake, decorate the edge with slices of dried apples or pears.

- Consider dipping the fruit in a sugar glaze and allowing it to solidify to give it a glittering appearance. Alternatively, add a little sparkle with crystallized fruits or lemon peel.

5. You should dust a plain cake with sifted cocoa or powdered sugar.

If you don't want to frost a cake that is already quite flavorful, use a fine mesh sieve or flour sifter over it. Fill it halfway with powdered sugar or cocoa powder and shake to coat the cake in sugar or cocoa powder.

Before dusting the cake, place a paper doily on top to create a lacy design. Then, carefully pull the doily away to reveal the ornamental pattern.

6. You have to garnish with chocolate drizzle, shavings, or pieces.

Chocolate is one of the most versatile cake decorations, as it may be used to create curls, shavings, chips, or chunks. For instance, use finely chopped white chocolate to create a fast border around the edge of the cake.

Additionally, you can melt a bar of chocolate and drizzle or pipe it over the cake. Create abstract designs or pipe a pattern with the chocolate.

7. Finish with a dollop of freshly whipped cream on the top.

Spoon whipped cream on top of the cake shortly before serving for a simple garnish that looks lovely with fresh fruit. If you want to pipe the whipped cream, you must first stabilize it with gelatin, marshmallow fluff, or pudding mix.

- Add a few drops of vanilla, almond, lemon, or coffee extract to the whipped cream to flavor it.

Tips

- Numerous hobby and craft stores offer classes in cake decorating.
- Experiment with decorating as many different types of cakes as possible. With each cake, you'll acquire experience and develop new skills.
- Tint your frosting or fondant to your desired hue. Add a few drops of food coloring and knead or mix until the desired color is achieved.
- Additionally, you can cut your cake into simple shapes and arrange them to make

more intricate forms and characters. For instance, you can make a Minnie Mouse cake by baking a rectangular cake and cutting out pieces for a face, two ears, and a bow.
- It is customary to showcase a decorated cake on a cake stand at parties and celebrations. You can also create your own cake stand to add a unique touch.

Warnings

- If you're coloring frosting using food coloring, keep in mind that the dye may stain your hands or clothing.
- Avoid adorning a cake with small hard candies if it will be served to small children, as the candies can cause choking.

Printed in Great Britain
by Amazon